10 Pennies for Jesus

Library of Congress Cataloging-in-Publication Data

Ward, Alton
        10 pennies for Jesus.

        Summary: Counting verses in rhyme describe the ways in which
monetary gifts for Jesus are used.
        1. Christian giving—Juvenile literature.
[1. Christian giving. 2. Counting] I. Mattozzi, Patricia, ill. II. Title.
III. Title: Ten pennies for Jesus.
BV772.W28   1986   248′.6 [E]   85-17140
ISBN 0-570-04132-5

1 2 3 4 5 6 7 8 9 10   PP   95 94 93 92 91 90 89 88 87 86

10 Pennies for Jesus

by Alton Ward
illustrated by Patricia Mattozzi

CONCORDIA

Publishing House
St. Louis

1 penny for Jesus.
Put it in the basket

To buy the Book we need:
A Bible we can read.

2 pennies for Jesus.
Put them in the basket

So part of what we give
Can help God's workers live.

3 pennies for Jesus.
Put them in the basket

To help the choir buy
Songs of God on high.

4 pennies for Jesus.
Put them in the basket

To learn of God's own Son
From leaflets that are fun.

5 pennies for Jesus.
Put them in the basket

For all that teacher brings,
Her books and everything.

6 pennies for Jesus.
Put them in the basket

God's house we want to build;
We pray it will be filled.

7 pennies for Jesus.
Put them in the basket

So we can help to feed
Those who are in need.

8 pennies for Jesus.
Put them in the basket

For those who have no clothes
For warmth in winter snows.

9 pennies for Jesus.
Put them in the basket

So each and everyone
Will learn what God has done.

10 pennies for Jesus. Put them in the basket

"All I have belongs to You.
Thank You, God, for all You do. Amen."

A NOTE TO PARENTS

Nursery-age children love putting their coins in the Sunday school collection basket. They know Jesus loves them, and they are thrilled to give Him something in return as a thank-you.

Though their understanding is limited, nursery-age children know that money has some sort of value and that people use it to buy things. They are unsure, however, what happens when they give money to Jesus. "Where does He keep it? Does He ever spend it? On what? Why does He need money if He can do miracles?"

10 Pennies for Jesus allows you the opportunity to explain what happens to our thank-offerings—and will help your child become excited about the Christian stewardship of money.

Because children learn best through participation, use ten real pennies as you read the book together. Let your child put the correct number of pennies on each page as it is read. Talk about the people in your congregation represented on each page, about the work they do, and how the money enables them to do their work *for Jesus*. The process will reinforce your child's ability to count and will help your child to understand one way she or he participates in the ministry of the church.

If your child is not enrolled in a Sunday school class, or, if your child's class does not take a collection, reinforce his or her stewardship participation by providing some coins that can be given in the church's collection. The process itself will help your child grow in stewardship skills and willingness.

Alton Ward